D1824799

Women's Work

Viv Quillin

Elm Tree books
London

this book is dedicated to
womens' work for peace

First published in Great Britain 1984
by Elm Tree Books/Hamish Hamilton Ltd
Garden House 57-59 Long Acre London WC2E 9JZ

Copyright © 1984 by Viv Quillin

British Library Cataloguing in Publication Data

Quillin, Viv
    Women's work.
    I . Title
    828'.91409   PN6175

    ISBN 0-241-11328-8

Printed and bound in Spain
by Grijelmo S.A., Bilbao

"I now pronounce you, HOUSE and WIFE."

MALE CHAUVINIST PIG and POOR COW IN NATURAL HABITAT..

Male Chauvinist Pig likes being in charge of someone, it makes him feel very important and strong.

Sometimes he gets tired of having to tell Poor Cow what to do, and cattle are not strong on companionship: But it's nice to have someone looking up to you - even if it's only a cow.

Poor Cow doesn't have to worry where the next mouthful of grass is coming from, but does get fed up with being put in the same field day after day.

She would pack her udder and leave, but who else would look after her?

Dear M.C.P.
I'm being rushed into hospital with heart attack. I've defrosted a casserole for you and there's rice pudding for afters. Sorry it's only tinned
love
P.C.
P.S. I'll be in intensive care but don't visit if you're tired.

The insurance Mrs G collected, enabled her to set up her own LAUNDERETTE and she is now going steady with the milkman.

WHICH JUST GOES TO SHOW

Some men are prepared to show willing at home, giving their partner a "helping hand" with the chores. This is a nice thing to do; Particularly if there are more than six children under five

mummy I feel **sick**

mummy where **are** you?

she's **hitting** me mummy

You want me to get your shopping in my **lunch break**?

Ms Powel
likes her secretaries
to have good legs.

THE SAGA of Beryl Tendon..

Beryl is twenty nine years old. She was brought up in a pleasant, middle-of-the-road family, and, (apart from the constant roar of traffic), had no more than the usual childhood traumas.

She always assumed she would marry a house and have 2·4 children.

But... seeing the skills required to do this i.e. patience of a saint, 24 hour stamina, devotion strong enough to surpass lack of pay, gratitude or prestige, she is now having second thoughts.

Maybe this is not her chosen calling after all, she enjoys her job, likes her friends....and yet...

to be continued...

FEBRUARY 6th

Board meeting 9.30
chairman Texoil 11am
lunch – Spanish Embassy
cut cats toenails
sausage and mash
tonight

I was going to do a film with
David Attenborough... but then
the kids came along...

THE CONTINUING SAGA
of Beryl Tendon..

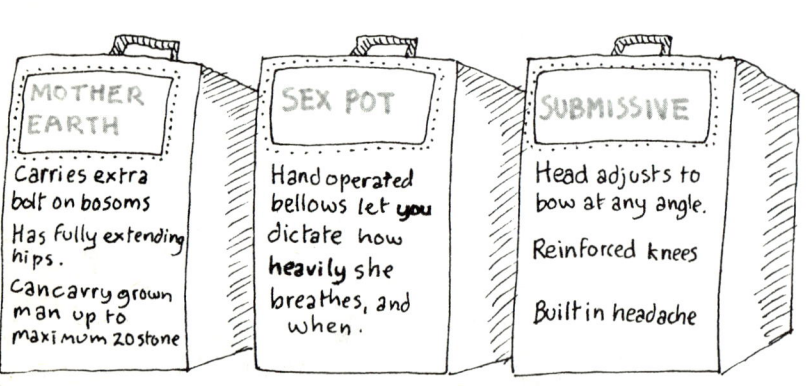

MEMO
_____

1.p.m. take
Mr Simpson of
Macho-Moguls
for lunch...

YET MORE SAGA
of
Beryl Tendon..

a woman was a **support**
to her man. . .

The Martyr

She is only happy when suffering which makes it very difficult for people around her to enjoy themselves unless they develop the hide of a rhinoceros.

On outings, she carries everybody's coats, picnics and Dad's fishing rod, saying, "Don't mind me - you run off and have a good time." The others dutifully skip about with a guilty feeling they can't quite fathom.

Gives up everything for others and is deaf to their pleas that they would rather she did not.

Enjoys poor health and usually lives a depressingly long time.

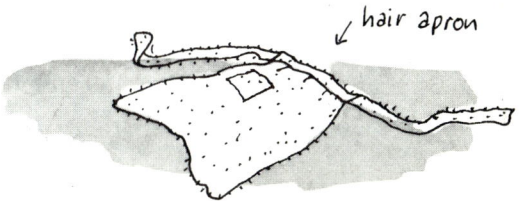
← hair apron

The Eternal Girl

Has eyes that open and shut, and says "Dada" if she falls over. Doesn't understand budgets, how to open doors, put her coat on, or big words.

Very enthusiastic with partner's cheque book. Has to be protected from horrid things like redundancy or illness, in case it upsets her.

Can turn nasty if people don't make her life lovely and nice and everything.

Possessive Sort

Knits boyfriend sweater with her name across the front. At work, has her initials carved on ruler, desk, chair and immediate floor area. Won't let anyone speak to the boss unless they've known him/her longer than she has: often becomes doctor's receptionist.

If she decides to take over a man, insists the wedding certificate is signed and witnessed by entire contents of church.

Husbands and children have to apply for a special pass to stay out after 6p.m, until they are old enough to leave home. After that it's extended to 8pm.

She tends to haunt from the grave, if bereaved husband isn't included on the funeral pyre

The Career Person

Refuses to do boss's shopping unless it's on a return basis. Has no sense of gratitude, i.e. constantly demanding promotion and wage rises. If these requests are not met, can be disloyal enough to go to another firm offering more.

Sneakily works long hours and then ruthlessly overtakes colleagues in senior positions. Speaks out at board meetings without waiting to be invited, and raises voice to strident pitch if interrupted.

Either wears feminine clothes to distract male staff, or-worse still-dresses severely in order to pretend she's a man.

Gets very petty if asked to pour the tea.

Would you like to be MOTHER — Miss Getty?

GLOSSARY OF TERMS

IN COMMON USE

FUTURE KITCHEN
mmm... just a hint of oregano, I think...
Keep the NOISE DOWN – it's 1 A.M.

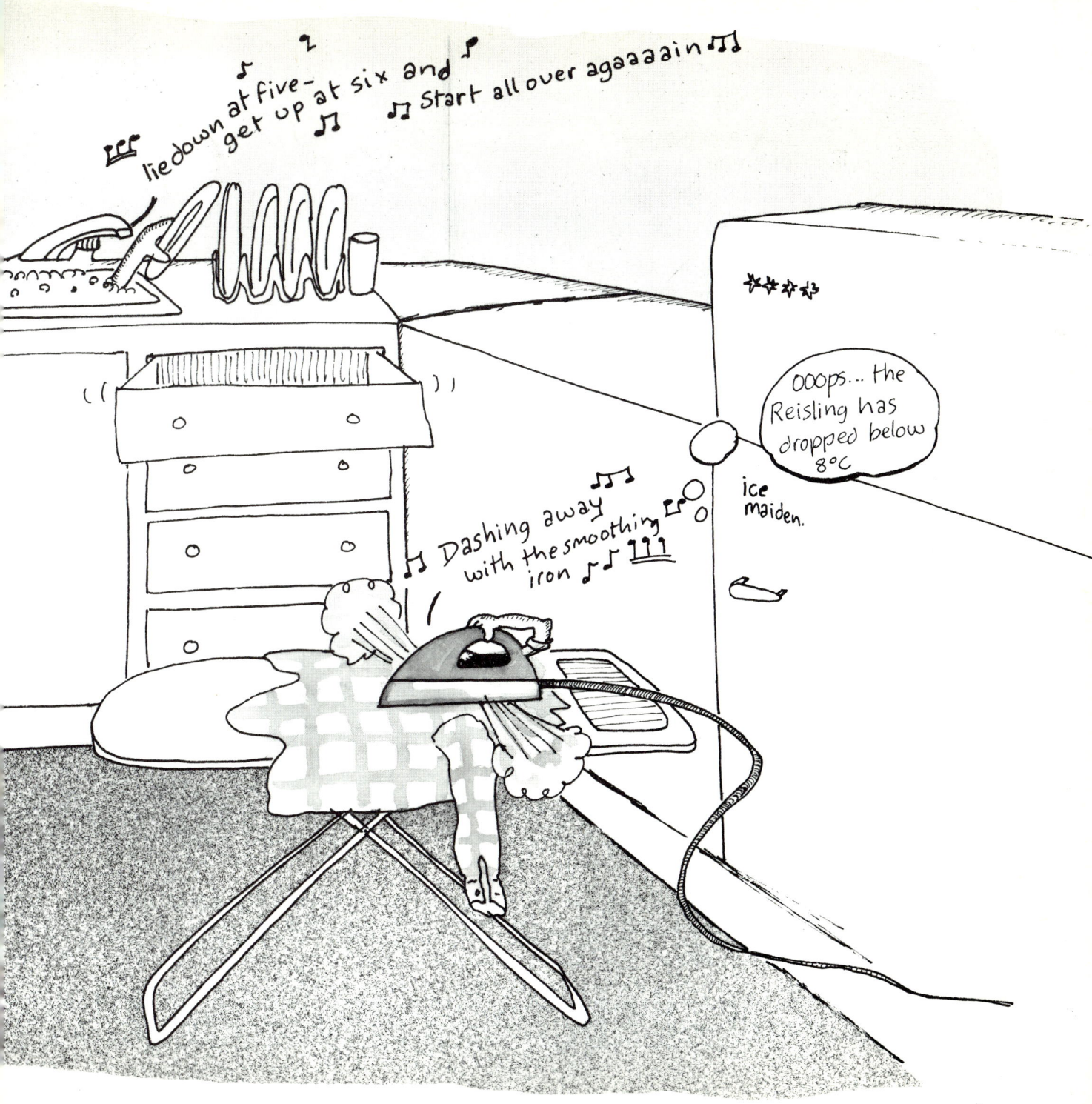

Break For Advertisement....

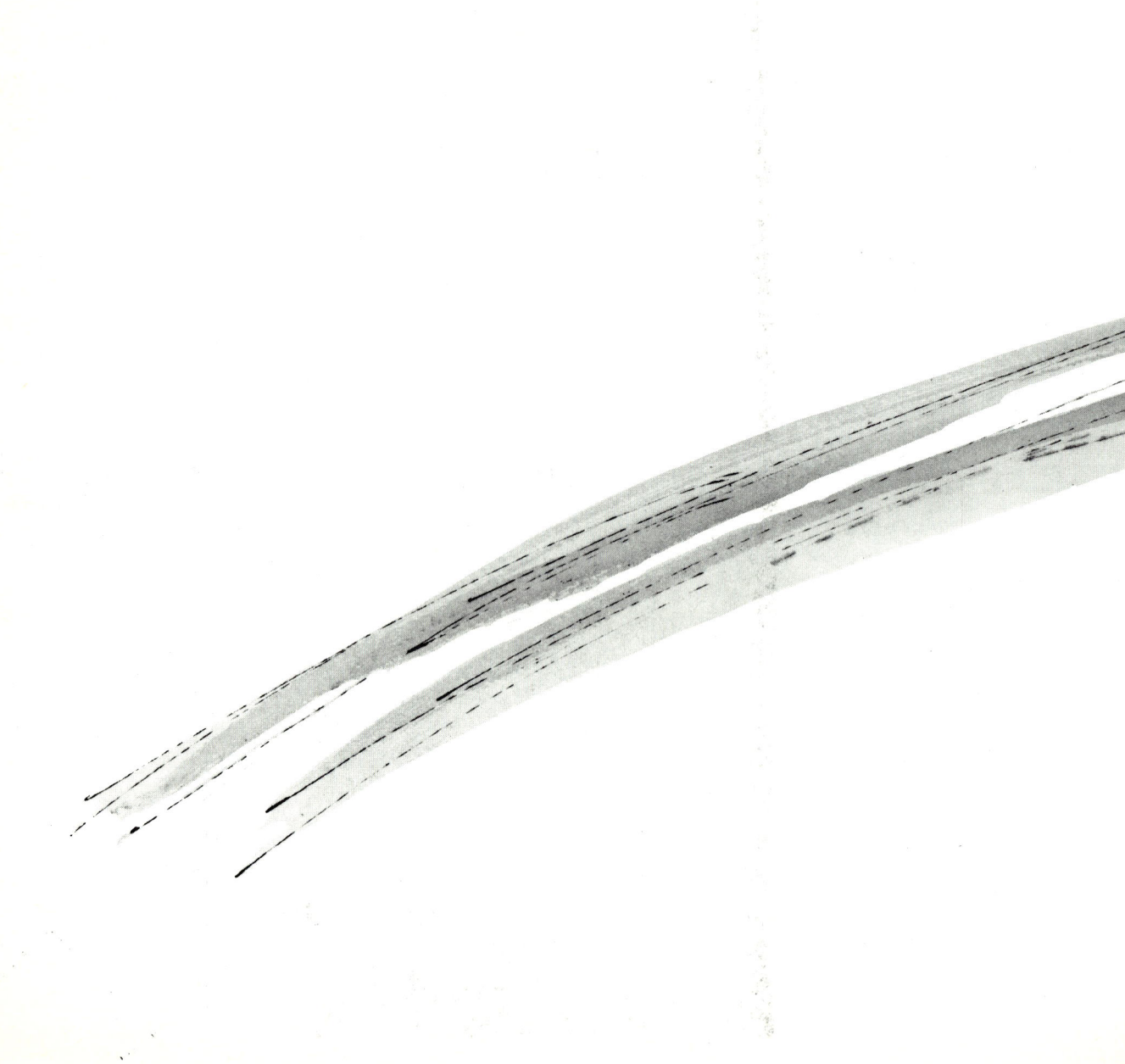

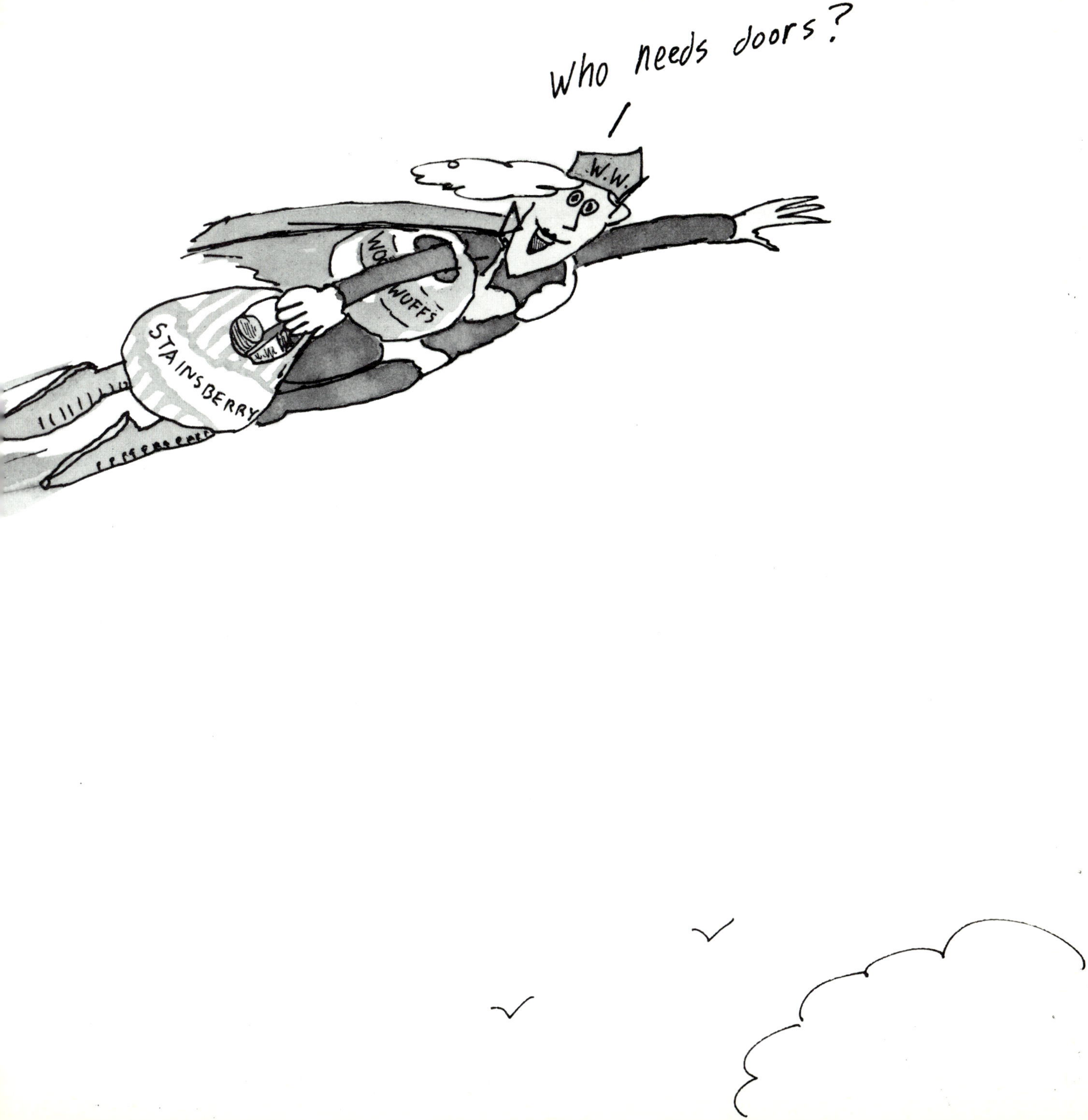
Who needs doors?
W.W.
WUFFS
STAINSBERRY

Viv Quillin was born in 1946 and semi-educated at a grammar school for gels.
    She has work experience in many areas including marriage, divorce, kids, drawing a bit and getting older.